❀ ❀ ❀ ❀ ❀ ❀ ❀ ❀ ❀ ❀ ❀

True Brit

❀ ❀ ❀ ❀ ❀ ❀ ❀ ❀ ❀ ❀ ❀

True Brit

The Story of Singing Sensation
Britney Spears

Beth Peters

BALLANTINE BOOKS • NEW YORK

This book contains an excerpt from the forthcoming paperback edition of *The Heat Is On* by Leah and Elina Furman. This excerpt has been set for this edition only and may not reflect the final content of the forthcoming edition.

A Ballantine Book
Published by The Ballantine Publishing Group
Copyright © 1999 by Beth Peters
Excerpt from *The Heat Is On* by Leah and Elina Furman copyright © 1999 by Leah Furman

Cover photo © Eddie Malluk/Retna

Ballantine and colophon are registered trademarks of Random House, Inc.

www.randomhouse.com/BB/

Library of Congress Catalog Card Number: 99-90436

ISBN 0-345-43687-3

Manufactured in the United States of America

First Edition: July 1999

10 9 8 7 6 5 4 3 2 1

To Pam K.,
who never stops singing . . .
and believing

❀Contents❀

❀Acknowledgments❀

Many thanks to all the interviewers, critics, friends, and neighbors who shared their insights and personal anecdotes of Britney. This book wouldn't have been possible without y'all. Also, thanks to my editor, Cathy Repetti, for her support; Robby, for hooking me up with the Kentwood locals; and my husband, who (as always) never complained when I burned the midnight oil (and dinner!) to meet my deadline. Love you, honey . . .

✿Introduction✿

When I was a little girl, my best friend Pammy and I used to sing along to Donny and Marie records and swear we were going to become the next great pop duo of the seventies.

Well, it didn't happen—maybe because neither one of us could carry a tune very well (and we never did decide who was a little bit country and who was a little bit rock and roll). But I remember fondly those early dreams of fame. Over the years, I've had my share of ups and downs professionally. I've lost a job, made some wrong decisions. But every time I felt discouraged, I thought back to those times when we pranced around my living room in purple socks singing along to the stereo. I refused to give up, and now—although I don't have a No. 1 single on the Billboard charts—I'm a successful writer covering (guess what?) the music industry. And I have a new role model, although I'm thirty and she's seventeen. Her name is Britney Spears.

Britney had childhood dreams, too, and she was determined to make them a reality, even when people told her she didn't stand a chance. Instead of becoming discouraged when she lost a role or blew an audition, she refused to lose hope. She tried new things, practiced hard, and held on tight.

Britney has a lesson for little girls—and big girls—everywhere: believe in yourself, and there's nothing you can't accomplish. Her record-breaking rise up the pop charts is living proof.

I remind myself of Britney's story every day when I crank up ". . . Baby One More Time" on my portable CD player. Thanks

Introduction

to Britney Spears, I walk a little taller (usually singing "Oh, baby, baby").

And who knows how far the road will take me.

—Beth Peters

True Brit

Chapter 1

❋Causing

a Commotion❋

"I hoped and prayed that this
would happen. I'm living my dream
and having the time of my life."
—BRITNEY SPEARS

Okay, maybe it seems like she material-
ized out of thin air: all of a sudden seven-
teen-year-old Britney Spears is at the top
of the charts, leaving Lauryn Hill, Foxy
Brown, Mariah Carey, even 'N Sync in
her dust. But the talented newcomer
didn't become this big overnight. She's
actually been polishing her act for the
past ten years, singing and dancing, she
has admitted, virtually since she was in

diapers. Her goal? Nothing less than superstardom—and that's exactly where she's headed.

Looking at the cover of her first CD, . . . *Baby One More Time,* you might find it hard to understand how she's rocketed to fame so fast: she looks just like any of the pretty girls you'd find in your local high school. But this small-town teen must have had something special that made her album sell over half a million copies in just a few short weeks. Try and figure it out and you'll be left scratching your head like most music critics. "She just has the right combination of looks, talent, drive," says *Billboard* magazine's radio editor Chuck Taylor. Or as her fans would prefer to call it, magic.

It started way back in 1987, when a little girl in pigtails was prancing around her Louisiana living room to Michael Jackson, singing into a can of hair spray. "Everyone thought I was just cute—I don't know how much they took me seriously when I said I was going to be a performer," Britney told MTV. Luckily, she believed in herself, and along the way, found great friends, advisers, and industry insiders who believed in her just as much.

But it's a long way from keeping the faith to becoming an international pop phenomenon, especially with all the competition that's out there. Every day, a new solo artist or band emerges to battle for the top of the charts, and veterans like Madonna and Cher still rule the airwaves. Britney has been compared to many of them.

"She has that Toni Braxton/Janet Jackson thing going in her voice," says Jane Stevenson, pop music critic for *The Toronto Sun*. But Brit insists she's nobody's imitator. Over the years, she's worked hard on stage, on screen, and in the studio to develop her own unique blend of pop jam. Sometimes funk, sometimes soul, sometimes hip-hop, even occasionally tinged with reggae rhythm, whatever she sings, she sings from the heart. And that, she will tell you, is what sets her apart.

3

Beth Peters

Once she had a sound, Britney needed the right image—and that's precisely what her label, Jive Records, has spent the last year perfecting. "She has this intriguing mix of personalities. Yes, she can be cute and wholesome, but just watch her video and there's definite sex appeal," says Danya Harpster, who interviewed Britney for *The New Orleans Times-Picayune*. Jive spent nearly six months marketing her before her single even hit record stores. Why? To create breathless anticipation for their new singing sensation. On January 12, 1999, the day her album was released, teens were already lined up at the crack of dawn to buy a copy. It's no wonder then, that . . . *Baby One More Time* debuted at No. 1, something virtually unheard of for a new artist, much less a female teenager.

The buzz began when Jive previewed Brit's single through a toll-free number connected to the direct-access music sampling line (callers heard "You Got It All" and "Sometimes" when they keyed in a four-digit code). When thousands of

Backstreet Boys fans bought their "Back-stage Pass" video (they're fellow Jive la-belers), they received a free CD sampler with Brit's "You Got It All" and "Soda Pop" on it. Sunglass Huts around the country handed out free cassettes of Britney and Imajin with a purchase; Hasbro's Interactive Girl Talk CD-ROM featured her tunes, and postcards were mailed out to record stores and pop fan clubs urging everyone to listen up. If you wanted to know more, you could check out Brit's very own web page at www.peeps.com/britney.

"The response was phenomenal," Chuck Taylor recalls. "And she hadn't even put out a song yet! If you got just a look at her, heard just a few minutes of her sound, you were hooked. Everything about this kid was infectious."

"It's music Top 40 can own," Clarke In-gram, production director of Rochester's WPXY radio, raved. "When Jive brought the record in and played it for me, I put it right into the mix."

Three months before her album was released, Brit began a twenty-eight-city tour of the malls of Middle America, sponsored by *YM*, *Teen*, *Seventeen*, and *Teen People* magazines. Hundreds of teens showed up at each performance to see her cut loose in a four-song set with two backup dancers. "They had no idea who I was yet," she told MTV. "But they liked my music." Lucky audiences even scored a cassette single and a Britney goody bag. She signed on to open for 'N Sync's concert tour, and since it ended in late January 1999, she's been taking her act outside of the United States to Canada, Europe, and Asia.

What's it like to catch her in action? Picture this: The Markville Mall in Toronto, Canada. Hundreds of kids are lined up to meet the girl who's inspired them to strut around their high school gyms crooning, "Oh, baby, baby." Britney breezes in— confident, waving, ready to meet and greet the masses. To brave the Canadian chill, she's dressed in funky bell-bottoms, a ski jacket, and a baby blue scarf (you can bet come school bell Monday morning, plenty of Canadian teens were copying this look as well). She smiles, she sings—she leaves 'em begging for more. "That was wild!" she screams, running off the stage. "That was totally amazing!"

But it was also just another day in the incredible life of Britney Spears.

Breakin' All the Records

According to *Billboard*, Brit was:

- the first new female artist to have a simultaneous No. 1 single in the Hot 100 and No. 1 album on the Billboard 200.
- the first new artist (male or female) to jump to the No. 1 spot on both the Hot 100 and Billboard 200.
- the first new artist (male or female) to have a single go to the No. 1 spot the same week that the album debuts at No. 1 on the Billboard 200.
- the first new female artist to have her first single and first album at No. 1 the same week.
- the youngest female in *Billboard* history to have a simultaneous No. 1 single and album debut at No. 1 in the same week.

It's also the first time in *Billboard* history that a single and album of the same name went to No. 1 simultaneously.

Chapter 2

❁The Little Girl
from Louisiana❁

Drive through Kentwood, Louisiana, population 2,400, and here's what you're likely to see: rolling hills, pine trees, haystacks, livestock, cornfields, and miles and miles of wide open spaces. The rooster down the road or the neighbor's mooing cow may be your alarm clock in the morning, and a night out on the town probably means a trip to the local burger barn. It's the kind of town where everyone knows everyone, and they greet you with a hearty "Hi, y'all!" when you walk through the door.

This was the town that Britney Spears grew up in, the largest in Tangipahoa

Parish, a small dairy community composed of warm, friendly southern folk who speak with a soft twang. The town was founded in 1891 and named after settler Amos Kent. Its claim to fame, locals will inform you, has been its sparkling clear springwater. And now, of course, they can add Britney Spears.

Britney is proud of her rural roots, and the town is equally proud of its famous citizen. "She really put Kentwood on the map and caused quite a stir," says Danya Harpster of *The New Orleans Times-Picayune*. "Suddenly reporters are calling, TV crews are coming. MTV is filming a day in the life."

But even though Britney's life has changed a great deal over the past two years, Kentwood has stayed the same. When Brit came back in mid-January 1999 en route to a concert in Baton Rouge, all her favorite hangouts were just as she had left them. There was Nyla's Burger Basket (her autographed picture hangs on the wall) and Sonic's Drive-In. How long had she patiently waited to turn fifteen and get her driver's license just so she could cruise on Highway 30 with her friends?

More than 250 town folk turned out at Kentwood Plaza to welcome her. "Many were close friends or neighbors who remembered her as a little girl," says Steve Byrd, editor of the weekly *Kentwood News Ledger*. "She's one of our own, and we watched her blossom here."

Born Britney Jeau Spears on December 2, 1981, she has always been "just a regular kid," say locals. Her mom, Lynne, is a second grade teacher at Spring Creek Elementary School; her dad, Jamie, is a building contractor who's often on the road. Their ranch-style house in Kentwood is "nothing fancy," says Byrd, who's visited often to interview Britney. "Lots of wood paneling inside with photos everywhere of the family; an easy recliner and fresh-cut flowers always on the kitchen table. Everyone comes in through the back door, which is often left wide open."

Friends at the Parklane Academy, a

small school in nearby McComb, Mississippi, that Britney attended, called her
"Bit-Bit," "Britty," or "Brit" for short, but
her mom preferred "Brinnie." Britney col-
lected dolls and Michael Jackson records
and loved riding up and down the dirt
roads in her go-kart. Brit, her parents, and
her two siblings—sister Jamie Lynne,
seven, and brother Brian, twenty-one—
were members of the Kentwood First Bap-
tist Church. That's where Britney studied
Bible in Sunday school and sang in the
choir. Her first "official" performance, she
recalls, was at age three at the Renee
Donewar School of Dance. Home photos
reveal a tubby toddler in tap shoes, a
tiara, and a gold lamé leotard receiv-
ing an award from Miss Renee for best
attendance.

Brit remembers fondly the day her mom
discovered she had real talent. She was
only about three years old and was
bouncing up and down on a trampoline
while singing in perfect pitch. "Mom took
me inside and had me perform for her.

She said, 'Brinnie, you can sing!' and that was like an instant boost for me."

Little Britney went on to become the star of her kindergarten graduation, performing a solo on the church stage. Being in the spotlight gave her confidence. (And as a little girl she was afraid of almost everything, from spiders to Santa Claus!) Soon sleepovers, birthday parties at Show Biz Pizza, and family trips to Disney World were mixed with ballet, tap, singing, and gymnastics lessons. "I'm really thankful to my parents," Brit has said. "Most parents are the ones pushing the child, but I was the one pushing them, and they supported me."

And her persistence paid off: the trophies and ribbons started to pile up. At age eight, she won her level at the Louisiana State Gymnastics meet, executing her now-famous back flips. In August 1990, she came in first place at the Kentwood Dairy Festival (she did a song and dance with a top hat and cane) and traveled to Baton Rouge for the Miss Talent Central States competition. There, say local newspapers at the time, she performed song, dance, and gymnastic routines to the song "I'm a Brass Band." She was selected the winner of her division (ages seven to nine) and overall winner (ages three to eighteen).

By now, Britney was getting used to the headlines. It seemed almost every week, she was earning another title or prize. She made front-page news a few years later in April 1992. At age ten, reported the *Kentwood News Ledger*, Britney Spears was crowned Miss Talent USA at the Monroe Civic Center. Singing and dancing to "There, I've Said It," she competed against seventeen other contestants from around the country. Her prize—along with a tiara, a banner, a four-foot-tall trophy, and a thousand-dollar check— would be two appearances on the national show *Star Search*. Her picture in the paper showed a beaming Britney standing next to the show's host, Ed McMahon. "Heeeere's Spears!" teased Ed.

Her neighbors weren't the slightest bit surprised by Britney's successes: Not only did she have talent, but she had tremendous drive and determination, even for her young years. Sure, she raised a few eyebrows over the years when she begged her mom to take her on auditions—even to strange cities.

"The amazing thing is this wasn't just a kid with big crazy dreams," editor Steve Byrd says. "Britney was actually making them come true."

Brit Brain Buster 1: Her Life, Her Loves

1. What song have both Britney and her little sis sung in church?
   a. "Silent Night"
   b. "What Child Is This?"
   c. "… Baby One More Time"

2. When she came home for Christmas 1998, what did Britney unexpectedly find at her back door?
   a. a present from the Kentwood Chamber of Commerce
   b. an adorable baby raccoon
   c. an obsessed male fan

3. What did Britney tell the *Minneapolis Star and Tribune* all her early training in performing failed to prepare her for?
   a. her career
   b. little sleep
   c. signing autographs

4. Who has Brit fervently denied having a crush on?
   a. Nick Carter of the Backstreet Boys
   b. Tom Cruise
   c. Mel Gibson

5. Who does Brit say are her "fashion idols"?
   a. Audrey Hepburn and Lauren Bacall
   b. Jennifer Love Hewitt and Jennifer Aniston
   c. The Spice Girls

Answers:

1. b; 2. c; 3. b; 4. a; 5. b

Hit Me One More Time...

For the 411 on Brit's birthplace (or even to visit) contact the Tangipahoa Parish Tourist Commission, 42271 South Morrison Blvd., Hammond, LA 70403; phone: 504–542–7520. They'll be happy to tell you about the local swamp walks, antique shops, museums, and charming bed–and–breakfasts in the area.

Chapter 3

❀Big Apple

Bound❀

When she was eight years old, Britney decided she wanted to audition in Atlanta for the Disney Channel's new *Mickey Mouse Club*. She has always loved watching the Mouseketeers, and being on TV sounded like the coolest job in the world. So her mom took her to an audition, and Brit sang her heart out, smiled, danced, and did cartwheels. Unfortunately, the producers thought she was just too young and inexperienced; most of the Mouseketeers were ages twelve to sixteen and had done more professional work.

But one of the casting directors liked what he saw and offered to help Britney secure an agent in New York. If she worked very hard, he told her, the next spot that opened up on the show might be hers. And besides, New York City was filled with opportunity for a talented little girl to break into showbiz.

"New York was a big move," she has said. "But it seemed like the center of everything." Her parents, she admits, weren't too enthusiastic at first. "My mom said, 'Brinnie, are you sure you want this?' Because it was unheard of. The people in town were saying to her, 'You're sending your daughter off to New York? Are you crazy?' "

But off she went—accompanied by her mom, Lynne, and her little sister, Jamie, who was then just a baby. Britney spent the next three summers studying at the Professional Performing Arts School (PPAS).

Founded in 1990, the school catered to kids who wanted to pursue professional work in the arts while they studied. Located on West 48th Street, it looked just like any other New York City public school with a big gray facade and "P.S. 17," the school's number, carved into the marble arch over the doorway. But once you walked past the red gate out front and stepped inside, the halls were filled with music. For admission into the school, potential students needed to audition—just as they would for a role. Brit studied vocal technique, music theory, and harmony, along with regular classes in subjects such as chemistry and algebra. Almost all the kids who went to PPAS felt exactly as she did: They wanted nothing more than to perform, and they took their career choice very seriously. Many of them were already accomplished entertainers, singing and dancing on Broadway or appearing in movies or TV series. It was the perfect environment for Britney to learn—not just academics, but all the ins and outs of show business.

After school, she practiced her pliés at Dance Center, a famous off-Broadway workshop, studying jazz, tap, and ballet. She landed a few national commercials (Mauls BBQ Sauce, Bell South, Days Inn) and off-Broadway shows, including 1991's

Ruthless!, a dark comedy based on the 1956 thriller *The Bad Seed*.

For eight months at the Players Theatre, Brit had the lead role in *Ruthless!* She played Tina Denmark, the seemingly sweet child who would do anything to be a star (Britney replaced Laura Bundy, the actress who had originated the role the year before). Written by Joel Paley with musical direction by Marvin Laird, the play was a musical farce that called for a kid who could ham it up and act like a dastardly diva. Brit was hilarious. She stood on a table, hair in perfect blond curls, and belted out, "I was born to amuse from the tip of my nose to the tap of my shoes!" The show's story cracked her up the first time she read the script: Tina is cast as a poodle named Puddles instead of the lead in a play. The only way to recast the role is to get rid of the leading lady . . . and Tina would kill (literally!) for that part.

The character, Britney has said, couldn't have been further from her real personality, but Tina was a lot of fun to play. "I got to be mean, spoiled, even evil!" she once reflected. "Then people would meet me afterwards and say, 'Wow! You're really nice after all.' "

New York was a completely different world from the one she had known in Louisiana. Instead of lush green hills, there were skyscrapers. While her sleepy little hometown rolled up the sidewalks in the early evening, there was always something new to do and see in New York City: shops, restaurants, plays, concerts, museums. The city bustled with excitement and possibilities. It seemed everyone wanted to be in showbiz (just judging from the number of people who showed up for every audition). Brit listened carefully when experienced actors gave her words of advice. Becoming a star, she discovered, wasn't as easy as she thought it would be. For some parts she was too young; for others she was too old. Some casting directors were looking for a brunette or a redhead, not a blonde. And some simply told her she wasn't the "right type"—whatever that type was. But not once did she get discouraged or worry that she wasn't good enough. Sure, there were lots of kids who were talented, but she had something many of them lacked: patience. Britney would keep practicing and auditioning, and she'd wait for her big break—because there was no doubt in her mind that would come. And she was right.

Theater 101

Before taking her bows off–Broadway, Britney had to learn these terms:

Ad–Lib To improvise lines that are not part of the script.

Call The notification to cast and crew of rehearsal or performance. This is also the countdown to the performance before the show. There's usually a half–hour call, a fifteen–minute call, a five–minute call, etc.

Cue To give actors a line when they have forgotten it or, a signal from the director to the cast or crew to start a scene, action, or dialogue ("Cue the dancing chorus girls!").

Dark theater A day or night when there is no performance.

Downstage The area of the stage closest to the audience.

Green room A backstage room used by actors and crew as a waiting area.

House The part of the theater where the audience sits.

Pit The area below the stage, usually where you'll find the orchestra.

"Places!" What the director yells when he wants the cast and crew to take their positions for the start of the performance.

Read–through The first rehearsal at which the company reads through the script.

Run The total number of performances for a production.

Run–through To rehearse the show from beginning to end without stopping.

Running crew The backstage people who perform all the technical tasks during the show.

Stage left The left side of a stage from the viewpoint of a person facing the audience.

Stage right The right side of a stage from the viewpoint of a person facing the audience.

Wings The right and left sides of the backstage area.

Hit Me One More Time . . .

❀

The script of *Ruthless!* is available from Samuel French, Inc., 45 West 25th Street, New York, NY 10010; phone: 212–206–8990.

Chapter 4

❀Club Kid❀

At age eleven, after honing her acting, singing, and dancing skills for three years, Britney felt she was finally ready to be a Mouseketeer. Only seven slots were open for new actors to join the already popular group of thirteen—and more than 15,000 kids showed up for the audition! After countless interviews over several days, producers called the list of names they had chosen: Christina Aguilera, Nikki Deloach, T. J. Fantini, Ryan Gosling, Tate Lynche, Justin Timberlake ... and Britney Spears! She had aced the audition and was given a contract for the next two seasons. The Club's creative team was impressed—this little girl had come a long way.

The first day Brit reported to the show's Disney World, Orlando, set for costume fittings and rehearsals, she could hardly contain her excitement. "It was so much fun," Brit told AOL's Entertainment Asylum. "I was like the baby on the show—only eleven or twelve—so people catered to me. But I wanted to work just as hard as everyone else."

"I remember this shining face who was ready to roll up her sleeves and get down to business," recalls Fred Newman, who hosted the new *Mickey Mouse Club* (renamed the much cooler *MMC*) during Britney's years on the show. It wasn't easy at first: The older kids with a few seasons under their belt were already sizing up the new class. Brit took a deep breath and forbade herself to have butterflies. This was the moment she had always dreamed about: Now everyone back home in Kentwood, not to mention the rest of the country, was going to see her every week

30

on TV! And she wasn't about to disappoint them.

"She was this powerhouse," Newman says. "She could just light up the screen, she had such a sparkle to her. And we all loved to have fun with her." In particular, Newman recalls playing a few pranks on Brit during those first weeks on the show. "It was sort of hazing—like her freshman orientation," he says. "At the beginning of the show, we'd all have to run out onstage. Just before it was Britney's turn, I'd pick her up over my shoulders, spin her around, then put her down. By the time she got out onstage, she was reeling!" Other times, he recalls with a laugh, they'd hold her dressing room door closed so she couldn't run out till just the last second—and she was huffing and puffing from trying to break it down!

Her mother, Lynne, Newman says, was doting and protective of her little girl, but not in a stage-mom sense. "They were a real family—not showbiz," he says. "She wanted Britney to have fun and learn, not just become rich and famous." During her two years with the 'Teers, Britney made a lot of great friends. Justin Timberlake from Memphis, Tennessee, and Christina Aguilera from Pittsburgh, Pennsylvania, were her closest pals (they were all about the same age). "Christina and I agree on everything," she told *Tutti Frutti Magazine* during her first season. "We like the same foods, doing the same things. If we see a boy and she thinks he's cute, I think he's cute!" Christina went on to describe Brit as "cheerful, innocent, and cute . . . She can always make me smile and feel good about myself." Says Newman, "Britney got along famously with everybody. By the second day, it was as if she had been with the show for six seasons—she was one of the club."

Britney's official press-kit profile for the show revealed some of her vivacious personality. Her goal, it said, was "to be a professional performer," and her hobbies were "playing basketball and riding her go-kart, shopping for classy clothes from the Gap, and getting together with family and friends for pizza (preferably pepperoni with a crunchy crust)." Her fave singer was Whitney Houston, and "Mel Gibson," she gushed, "is real cute!"

During the show's sixth season—Brit's first—the cast shot thirty-six episodes in April through October, to air October through December 1993. Britney got to appear in several numbers and skits, including "Love Can Move Mountains," "Gonna Have a Good Time," "Don't Walk Away," "Strict Mom," "I Feel for You," "Yecch!," "Step to da Rhythm," and "Elvis Today." There were always great celebrity guests—Jeremy Jordan, Brian McKnight, SWV, Shai, Scott Weinger, Jenna Von Oy, Gabrielle Carteris, and Brian Austin Green. Each show had a different theme. On Party Day, Guest Day, Hall of Fame Day, and Music Day, Britney got to dress up in goofy outfits and wigs, tell jokes, and sing and dance. Sometimes she was even allowed to sign off the show with an enthusiastic "See you real soon!"

By her second season, performing on the show was a breeze. Each week, Britney was given a production schedule and script. Roles were written and then assigned. It was always the producer's final decision, but the music director and choreographer had a say in what 'Teer could appear in a scene. Britney was always a popular choice: She memorized her lines like a pro, picked up the choreography in the first run-through, and belted out each number with perfect pitch. Between takes, she played Ping-Pong and hung out with the audience, offering words of wisdom about performing to *MMC* wanna-bes. There were a few new members joining up and she made them feel right at home—she remembered what it was like to be the new kid on the block. That season, they shot forty-four episodes, airing from May 4, 1995, to March 7, 1996. In the United States, a new episode ran every Thursday and repeated on Sunday—just in case you needed a double dose of Brit and the rest of the 'Teers.

The Disney Channel canceled *MMC* in January 1997. The producers were disappointed with the ratings, and at the same time, many of the Mouseketeers were about to graduate from high school, and most of them wanted to go to college or move on to other projects. They were all released from their contracts. Today, if you're lucky enough to live in Canada, you might be able to catch Season Seven episodes on the Family Channel. The popularity of 'N Sync and Britney had Canadian viewers begging for reruns.

"It was an incredible group," Newman says, also citing former 'Teer Keri Russell, star of the WB's *Felicity*. "They were all so talented that when the show ended, I knew we hadn't seen the last of this crew."

___Whatever Happened to Brit's MMC Bunch?___

Albert: croons tunes
He is a background singer for Kirk Franklin.

Blain: married man
He works with computers and is living in Arizona with his wife and son. The only married *MMC*-er to date.

Braden: lying low
Last seen on *MMC* in 1989.

Brandy: serious student
Attending the University of South Alabama in Mobile, Alabama.

Chase: creating a buzz
He's the lead singer of the group Buzzfly.

Christina: future diva
"Reflection," her song on the *Mulan*

soundtrack, is a huge hit, and she's releasing her debut album.

Dale: what's up, doc?
Recently played a medical student on *ER* and is appearing in the movies: *Cold Hearts* is due out spring 1999 and *Random Shooting in L.A.* will be released later in the year.

Damon: commercial appeal
Living in California and was last seen in some advertisements in early 1998.

David: stage star
He played the part of Thuy in *Miss Saigon* in 1997.

Deedee: gives her regards to Broadway
She recently played the lead, Kim, in *Miss Saigon* and did a stint on the soap *As the World Turns*.

Ilana: Big Apple babe
She's currently in New York City, studying acting at famed Lee Strasberg Theater Institute.

Jason: move over, Garth
He's in Nashville recording a country album.

J.C.: 'N Sync-ronized, part 1
He's one-fifth of the hot group—need we say more?

Jennifer: bright lights, big city
She is currently working on an album while attending school in New York.

Josh: booking it
He's also attending school in New York.

Justin: 'N Sync-ronized, part 2
Who knew he and J.C. would still be hanging together?

Keri: TV's new "It" girl
Starring in the WB series *Felicity* and in the upcoming movie *Mad About Mambo*. She recently won a Golden Globe Award.

Kevin: sun, sand, and surf
He's working in Southern California.

Lindsey: college coed
She's attending the University of Missouri.

Marc: Big Mac attack
Has been heard doing McDonald's commercials (voice–over) and seen making guest appearances on TV.

Matt: like father, like son
He's attending college in Tennessee and touring with his father, country singer Gary Morris.

Mowava: heavenly role
Last seen on *Touched by an Angel* in early 1998.

Mylin: a CD-to-be
She recently signed to a record label and will have an album out in the next year.

Nikki: *Achtung,* baby!
She's part of the group Innosense, who are currently promoting in Germany.

Nita: beauty queen
She was crowned Miss Virginia after the winner of the pageant was crowned Miss America (Nita was first runner-up).

Rhona: looking for a label
Rumored to be in California working on a debut album with fellow *MMC*-er Tony Lucca.

Ricky: ghostly gig
He's living in Los Angeles and was last seen in a small part in the 1998 made-for-video movie *Casper Meets Wendy*.

Roque: boy in a band
Last mentioned in a 1996 interview with Lindsey as being in a music group.

Ryan: Greek god
Stars as Young Hercules in the Fox series.

Tasha: in vogue
Has been doing some modeling and is working as a host for an educational CD–ROM.

Tate: class act
He's in his senior year of high school in Florida.

Terra: city slicker
She recently moved to New York City and was last seen in a commercial in 1995.

T.J.: sleepless in Seattle
He's cramming for exams at Cornish College of the Arts in Seattle.

Tiffini: still on screen
Last seen in a commercial in 1997.

Tony: double disks
He's currently promoting his second independent album.

Hit Me One More Time . . .

For the latest news on the 'Teers, check out this extensive unofficial fan site, The All New Mickey Mouse Club Online, at www.multiboard.com/~spettit/mmc/.

Chapter 5

❋Welcome Back,
Britney!❋

Almost immediately after the *Mickey Mouse Club* was canceled, Britney went home to Kentwood. Why not take time to enjoy her teenage years? she reasoned. She missed her best buddies and just hanging out at home with her family. Besides, it would give her time to evaluate her next move: Would she take on another TV series or play . . . or maybe something entirely new?

Back home, no one treated her any differently, even if she was a TV star now. The town had known a few famous folk before her—two professional football players, Michael Jackson and Jackie Smith, graduated from Kentwood High—

and if Britney wanted to resume her normal life, they were happy to have her.

"She was always down-to-earth, sweet, polite, unaffected," says Steve Byrd of the local paper. "She made it sound like it was no big deal that she'd been away for a while making a name for herself. It was her choice to come back, and everyone welcomed her."

Brit attended a private high school for a full year in McComb, Mississippi, always acing her social studies, English, and science classes. (Math, however, wasn't her forte!) She went to sock hops and read Sweet Valley High novels; she even had a steady boyfriend. Weekends were spent cramming for tests and going to the movies or the mall with her cousin Laura Lynn and close friends. Kentwood, of course, was too small to have a mall or a theater. The nearest shopping centers were half an hour away in Hammond or Baton Rouge, and New Orleans was almost an hour away.

Brit visited with her grandparents at

their local business, Granny's Seafood (the house specialty was boiled crawfish), and pinned pictures of Tom Cruise to her bedroom walls. She tossed sticks for her rottweiler, Cane, and played b-ball and watched Chicago Bulls games with her big bro. It was comfortable and cozy to spend time with the people she knew and loved. But something, Britney couldn't help feeling, was missing.

"I did the homecoming and prom thing and I was totally bored," she confessed to *People*. "Every weekend we'd do the same things. It was fun for a while, but I started getting itchy to get out again and see the world."

Lynne sensed her daughter was anxious. So when Britney turned fifteen, her mother sent Britney's homemade demo tape to New York entertainment lawyer Larry Rudolph. From the first listen, he knew he had a hit on his hands and signed on as her co-manager. (Brit's other manager is Johnny Wright, who steered the careers of New Kids on the Block and the Backstreet Boys.)

Beth Peters

Rudolph wanted Britney to return to New York and meet a group of record execs. They'd love her, he assured Lynne Spears. All Britney had to do was be herself.

What's She Really Like?

According to friends and neighbors:

Polite: She says "Yes, ma'am," "No, sir," and "Thank you, ma'am" when speaking to adults.

Tiny: Brit stands about five feet four and weighs about 108 pounds. The boys in 'N Sync swear they can bench-press her!

Playful: She likes to kid around with pals, build sand castles at the beach, and tease her little sister, Jamie, mercilessly.

Bighearted: Brit will never say no to a fan who asks for her autograph. She'll also always stop and pose for pictures.

Down-to-earth: Britney is no prima donna. Even though she's a huge star, she makes no demands (except for extra cheese on her pizza!).

A shopaholic: While hitting the malls to promote her album, Brit just loved to browse in stores coast to coast!

Très athletic! Those in the know will testify that the girl has abs of steel. She can also do cartwheels, back flips, and shoulder-high scissor kicks (her dancers swear she can do splits as well). And she's been known to beat the pants off her big brother at one-on-one hoops.

Friendly: When visiting radio stations 'round the country, Brit not only met DJs and station managers, but actually walked around shaking hands and saying hello to everyone who worked there.

Kindhearted: Brit has said she'd like to get involved with some great causes. Since she loves animals so much, that might turn into her "pet" charity.

A Few of Her Favorite Things

Ice Cream: cookie dough
Food: pizza, hot dogs, pasta with tons o' sauce
Cereal: Cocoa Puffs
Drink: Sprite ("has to be fizzy, not flat")
Weekend activities: shopping (according to her official Jive bio, she loves "colors that pop and shopping till you drop"), catching a flick, riding her go-kart, soaking in the rays at the beach
Sports: b-ball, golf, swimming, and tennis
Stores: Bebe, A/X, the Gap, XOXO, Scoop, Todd Oldham, the Store
Color: baby blue
Flower: roses, preferably white ones
School subject: English, "because there's a lot of reading and writing"
Movies: _My Best Friend's Wedding_ and _Steel Magnolias_ (obviously, she's a big Julia Roberts buff!)
Cartoon character: Goofy

At-home hobbies: reading romance novels, collecting dolls, rooting for the Chicago Bulls and the New York Yankees on TV

Type of guy she goes for: long–haired and rugged, "not the pretty boy type at all"

Heartthrobs: Ben Affleck ("I'd love to go out with him!"), Tom Cruise, Mel Gibson, Brad Pitt

TV show: Dawson's Creek

Musicians: Natalie Imbruglia, Lenny Kravitz, matchbox 20, Mariah Carey, Whitney Houston, Prince, Brandy, Third Eye Blind, Aero-smith, BSB

Song: Prince's "Purple Rain"

Book: The Horse Whisperer

Animal: puppy dogs

Expressions: "That's sweet!" "Awe-some!"

Hit Me One More Time . . .

❀

For more of the inside scoop on Britney's personal faves, check out these
unofficial fan sites (these people are seriously up on every intimate detail):

www.geocities.com/Sunset Strip/
   Club/9204
www.crosswinds.net/toronto/
   ~britpass
www.angelfire.com/nc/
   unofficialbritney
www.geocities.com/Sunset Strip/
   Stadium/5524
www.gurlpages.com/music/bspears/
   enter.html
listen.to/britney_jeau_spears
members.tripod.com/~QuikBunny/
members.tripod.com/britneyonline/
members.tripod.com/~bspears/
   index.htm

Chapter 6

❀A New Direction❀

So one more time, Brit trekked back to the Big Apple. This time, though, there was a great deal more than just a small role in a series or play at stake. "Being a pop singer is what I always wanted to do since I was a little kid," she told *The Toronto Sun*. "I used to dance around to Whitney and Prince and think, 'I could do this!'" Sure, she had a lot of experience on stage and TV, but this was an entirely new dream to pursue. Did she have what it would take? Attorney Rudolph seemed to think she had the makings of a new Mariah Carey. Now all she had to do was convince the recording industry.

The buzz in the biz was that several labels were looking for a new teen queen. The Recording Industry Association was estimating that teen-geared acts were accounting for 10 percent of all pop albums sold in the country. Not since the early and mid-eighties had as many preteen and teen fans (ages nine to sixteen) been spending so much on music.

"The time was right," says *Billboard*'s Chuck Taylor. "The youth pop movement was big, with boy bands like the Backstreet Boys and 'N Sync. There was an opening for a young female to do the same thing."

That person would need a great deal more than just vocal talent. Labels were looking for a girl who had personality and style. She had to be able to carry a tune and sell lots of albums as well. This next superstar had to be someone girls would want to emulate and boys would want to date, the perfect combination of sweetness and sex appeal.

Rudolph was convinced Britney was all that and more. He sent her on an audition for an all-girl group, and just as he had predicted, she wowed them. Record execs saw star potential. Britney was too dynamic a singer and dancer to be part of a trio or foursome; she could command a stage all by herself. With that encouragement, she began devoting herself full-time to a solo career, working hard in the studio on demos while studying several hours each day with tutors to keep up with her high school requirements.

Rudolph sent a one-song demo to Jeff Fenster, a senior vice president at Jive Record Label. "I heard something special," Fenster told *Billboard*. "She sang over an instrumental that wasn't even in her key, but her vocal ability and commercial appeal caught me right away."

Next came an impromptu audition for several Jive executives. "It was nerve-racking," Britney told *The Calgary Sun*. "I'm used to singing in front of big crowds and I went in there and there were these ten executives sitting and staring at me." Brit just closed her eyes and gave it her best shot—and it worked. The reaction was unanimous: Jive asked her to sign a record deal, and she jumped at the chance.

"She's got edge," Jive president Barry Weiss declared to the *New York Daily News*. "Our view is that she's a young Madonna." (Brit, by the way, loved the compliment: "I totally respect and admire how every time Madonna comes out, she grows as an artist," she told America Online.) Jack Slatter, senior vice president of pop promotion at Jive, deemed Britney "a very special artist . . . with longevity."

The record label was behind her 100 percent, and was eager to pair her with talented writers, musicians, and producers who would help her find her own unique sound. She would get to work with Eric Foster White, who had produced and written material for Whitney Houston, Boyzone, Regina Belle, Hi-Five, and others. Fenster assured her that she'd be as big as those artists and that he'd assemble a great team to make it happen.

Of course, her advisers warned her, the comparisons would be inevitable: Any young girl brave enough to stake her claim in the pop music scene would find herself labeled a teenybopper Tiffany or Debbie Gibson. But Britney was ready for it. She had a mature, soulful voice that would blow away any such prejudgments. "I'm my own person," she told Canadian reporters while trying to remain diplomatic. "I don't think I sound like anyone except me, but to be compared to other singers who have a lot of talent, that's got to be a compliment."

Girl Power

Like Brit, these young females went to the top of the charts.

Tiffany

This Norwalk, California, teen made her mark with mall appearances, whipping the kid crowds into a frenzy. She had two consecutive No. 1 singles in the eighties—"I Think We're Alone Now" and "Could've Been"—from her 1987 quadruple-platinum debut album, _Tiffany_. Her 1988 album, _Hold an Old Friend's Hand_, launched the Top 10 single "All This Time" and went platinum, but after that, fickle fans deemed her yester-day's news.

Debbie Gibson

At the age of seventeen, Debbie be-came a pop phenomenon in the late eighties, producing five Top 5 singles, including two No. 1s, and two multi-platinum albums. While still in high school, she signed with Atlantic Records and began recording her debut album, *Out of the Blue*. It was released in the fall of 1987, and by the spring of 1988, it had reached the Top 10. The title track became a No. 3 hit and was followed by her first No. 1 single, "Foolish Beat," making her the youngest artist ever to write, perform, and produce a No. 1. "Lost in Your Eyes," the first single from her second album, *Electric Youth*, became Debbie's biggest hit early in 1989, staying at No. 1 for three weeks. She continued to release a few albums in the mid–1990s, but none sparked any fireworks with fans. Now calling herself Deborah, this Gibson girl refuses to give up. She's turned her talents to the stage, appearing on Broadway in *Les Misérables* and *Beauty and the Beast*.

Robyn
The twenty–year–old Swedish songbird rocks her homeland with a mix

of American R&B and ABBA–esque pop. Her single, "Do You Know (What It Takes)," went Top 10 around the world, including the United States. Robyn wrote her first song at the age of eleven and was discovered a few years later when performer Meja heard her singing during a concert intermission. Meja got her a record contract with Sweden's Ricochet Records. In 1995, when she was only sixteen, Robyn began recording her debut album with Max Martin, and *Robyn Is Here* quickly soared to the top of the Swedish charts. The album hit the States almost a year and a half later, and is proving just as popular on distant shores.

Mya

Last year, at age eighteen, this smooth urban R&B artist demonstrated she had mainstream appeal as well. Mya started out as a dancer. In her preteens, she joined the troupe T.W.A. (Tappers With Attitude). She left the group after a short time and came to New York to study at the Dance Theater of Harlem with Savion Glover, the brains behind Broadway's *Bring in Da Noise, Bring in Da Funk.* She then set her sights on singing, and convinced Interscope Records to sign her. Mya's debut album, *It's All About Me,* was released in April 1998 and is still scoring in both the R&B and pop markets.

Hit Me One More Time . . .

❁

Books on the music biz (in case, like Brit, you're bent on breaking in)

All You Need to Know About the Music Business by Donald Passman (Simon & Schuster, 1997). Penned by an expert entertainment lawyer who's been there, seen that.

How to Be a Working Musician: A Practical Guide to Earning Money in the Music Business by Mike Levine (Watson–Guptill, 1997). How to get started, from singing in local clubs to landing jingles in commercials.

Networking the Music Business by Dan Kimpel (Writer's Digest, 1993). The art of the schmooze by an advertising director for the L.A. Songwriter's Showcase. How to make contacts with the players.

The Real Deal: How to Get Signed to a Record Label from A to Z by Daylle Deanna Schwartz (Watson–Guptill, 1997). A commonsense guide to launching a recording career and landing a label.

Chapter 7

One Single Sensation

Once she signed on the dotted line and Jive recruited a crew, Britney was ready to embark on the actual recording of her first single and album. She divided her recording sessions between two studios: Eric Foster White's in New Jersey and Sweden's Cheiron Productions in Stockholm. In Sweden she would be paired with Max Martin, a brilliant writer and producer who had worked with Backstreet Boys, Ace of Base, and Robyn.

As her airplane soared into the clouds, Britney had to pinch herself to make sure she wasn't dreaming. She was going on her first trip abroad, to Sweden, to make an album that Jive promised her would fly up the charts.

"It was so exciting," she recalled. "But also a little scary." After all, she was meeting so many new faces and visiting new places. She promised herself, just as in her MMC days, she wouldn't let anyone see that her knees were knocking a little. She'd be cool and confident and prove that even though she was only fifteen, she was a pro.

Max Martin met Britney at the studio. He had never heard of this bubbly young girl from the States, but the minute she sang just a few notes of his music, he was convinced she would be the next big thing. He originally had agreed to do two songs with her, but after just one listen, Martin decided to do eight of the eleven on the album.

"She's got an excellent voice with a bit of flavor in it," he has said. "She has a good sense of catching the melody and taking it to another level." Britney blushed when Martin compared her to Robyn and the Backstreet Boys. If he thought she was *that* good, well then, she would just have to be!

Britney worked hard for an entire year, turning sweet sixteen in the process. She recorded track after track, over and over, and worked with White and Martin to get just the right emotion in her voice to give the songs depth and meaning. She couldn't just sing them—she had to feel them as well.

"Even if I haven't necessarily experienced every emotion in my music, I can relate," she revealed during an online chat. "I had a serious boyfriend for two years and we broke up. I thought I was in love—I guess I was at first, because he was my world. But it got to be too much." And, she insists, the memory of their split still hurts. "You don't just forget it. I think any girl my age can understand and maybe have felt the same way at some point."

Watching both of her mentors, White and Martin, in action, she was inspired to pen her own music as well. "At the end of the year, I started writing a lot," she told *The Tennessean.* "It's something I want to do, definitely." The B side of her second single, "Sometimes," features a Spears original. "I'm proud of it," she said. "And when the next album comes along, hopefully I can do more."

The song she loved the most on this CD was one of Martin's, ". . . Baby One More Time." "I had been in the studio for about six months, listening to and recording music," she told *Billboard.* "I hadn't really heard a hit yet. Then Max played me the demo, and it blew me away. It just felt really right." Brit went into the studio and recorded ". . . Baby One More Time," adding "a little more attitude" than the original demo. She liked it so much—and so did Martin—that it became the title of the entire CD and the first single off the album. That single would be released in the United States on October 23, 1998, followed by the album's release in January. The CD would be "enhanced," so that when it was played on a CD-ROM drive, it would include exclusive backstage interviews, videos, and personal photos from Brit's scrapbook.

It all sounded like a winning formula, but neither Martin nor Brit could predict what critics would have to say about the single's lyrics. A few questioned the message behind the music. "Some people took it that some violence or S&M is implied when this girl is asking her boyfriend to hit her one more time," points out *The Toronto Sun*'s Jane Stevenson. Brit shrugs off the suggestion. "She means hit her with a sign," she told the paper. "I think people are reading a lot more into it."

Of course any artist who churns out an album has to be prepared for criticism. "You put yourself out there, so yes, people do look you over and pass judgment," she has said. "But that comes with the territory. The more popular you become, the more people talk about you."

But Britney wasn't prepared for all the attention to start so quickly. She was heading home to Kentwood in fall 1998 for some time with her family, climbing into a car after her long flight. "I turned on the radio, and there was my voice and my single," she recalled. "I was totally freaking out! It was the best feeling."

". . . Baby One More Time" picked up 2,789 spins on mainstream Top 40 radio for the week of November 8, 1998, according to Broadcast Data Systems. Translation? It was a huge hit and became the No. 1 most-added-track to radio station playlists during its first week of release.

Stations couldn't keep up with the requests. "It all happened so fast," Brit told MTV. "It's really flattering. It feels great when you see fans getting into your music, and you know that your instincts had been right all along."

Globe/Mark Allen

Retna/Paniccioli

"She's got edge!"

"She had such a sparkle to her."

"If you just got a look at her, heard just a few minutes of her sound, you were hooked."

"Someone the girls would want to emulate and the boys want to date."

"I'm still Britney Spears from Kentwood, Louisiana."

All photos Globe/Mark Allen

"She's America's teen sweetheart."

Globe/Mark Allen

Retna/Granitz

Top of the Pop

Here are Brit's chart positions since her single and CD were released.

"... Baby One More Time" (single), according to _Billboard_

Week of	Position	Week of	Position
11/21/98	17	1/16/99	4
11/28/98	14	1/23/99	3
12/5/98	18	1/30/99	1
12/12/98	9	2/6/99	1
12/19/98	8	2/13/99	2
12/26/98	5	2/20/99	2
1/2/98	4	2/27/99	4
1/9/98	4	3/6/99	5

... _Baby One More Time_ (album), according to _Billboard_

Week of	Position	Week of	Position
1/30/99	1	2/20/99	1
2/6/99	3	2/27/99	1
2/13/99	2	3/6/99	1

". . . Baby One More Time" (airplay of single), according to American Top 40

Week of	Position	Week of	Position
10/17/98	39	1/9/99	5
10/21/98	25	1/16/99	7
11/7/98	20	1/23/99	8
11/14/98	17	1/20/99	7
11/21/98	12	2/6/99	5
11/28/98	12	2/12/99	2
12/5/98	8	2/20/99	1
12/12/98	8	2/27/99	1
12/19/98	5	3/6/99	1

Fellow Labelers

Britney is in good company at BMG (home of Peeps and Jive):

Whitney Houston	Reel Tight
Naughty by Nature	III Frum Tha
Outkast	Soul
R. Kelly	Andrea Martin
Imajin	Levi Little
Keith Murray	Wild Orchid
Christina Aguilera	P.M. Dawn
(fellow _MMC_–er)	A Tribe Called
Jerome	Quest
Baby DC	E–40
Deborah Cox	Funkmaster
112	Flex
Backstreet Boys	Mase

Brit Brain Buster 2: Her CD

1. Who *doesn't* Brit thank on her CD?
   a. God
   b. her family
   c. the gang at Nyla's Burger Basket
   d. her lawyer

2. What image appears on the CD?
   a. the initials B.S.
   b. a flower
   c. a soda pop
   d. a baby

3. In what year was Sonny and Cher's *The Beat Goes On* originally released?
   a. 1967
   b. 1957
   c. 1975
   d. 1980

4. In what foreign city were several of Britney's songs recorded and mixed?

a. Stockholm, Sweden
b. Paris, France
c. London, England
d. Tokyo, Japan

5. On what soundtrack album does Brit's "Soda Pop" appear?
   a. *Ally McBeal*
   b. *Baywatch*
   c. *Sabrina, the Teenage Witch*
   d. *Touched by an Angel*

6. Approximately how many total minutes of music are on the CD?
   a. 41
   b. 60
   c. 22
   d. 86

7. How many songs are on the CD?
   a. 10
   b. 8
   c. 11
   d. 13

8. What is *not* the name of one of Brit's tunes?
   a. "I Will Still Love You"
   b. "Sometimes"
   c. "E-mail My Heart"
   d. "Born to Love You"

9. On what day did Brit's album hit U.S. stores?
   a. January 24
   b. January 12
   c. December 24
   d. February 1

10. Who designed the tank top Britney is wearing on the CD cover?
    a. Armani X-change
    b. Tommy Hilfiger
    c. Todd Oldham
    d. Betsey Johnson

Answers:

1. c; 2. b; 3. a; 4. a; 5. c; 6. a; 7. c; 8. d; 9. b; 10. a

Hit Me One More Time . . .

Follow Brit's reign 'round the world
with these websites:

Australian Music Charts
  www.hitsquad.com/amc/

Top 30 International
  www.rve.marche.it/classifiche/
  international.htm

Charts All Over the World
  www.lanet.lv/misc/charts/

Irish Top 30
  www.2fm.ie/music/charts/
  singles.cfm

British Top 40
  www.mfmradio.co.uk/top40/

German Top 20
  www.tmf.nl/data/charts/top40/
  index.htm

Swedish Top 20
  www.sr.se/stockholm/musik/
  topp20.htm

Chapter 8

❀Just One
of the Boys❀

The time: January 1999. The scene: The Riverside Centroplex in Baton Rouge, Louisiana. A sold-out crowd of 8,799 fans—mostly girls—are screaming and waving homemade signs: "Lance, I Love You!," "Joey rules," "J.C. + Me," "Justin, I'm lustin' 4-U!" Following the opening act by the all-girl band B*Witched, concert emcee Johnny White leaps onstage to announce the concert's special guest. "She's the hometown girl who's made it big!" And suddenly the eager audience begins to chant "Britney! Britney!" And leading the cheers, right up front, is her entire family who've come to see her tonight.

81

Backstage, Britney beams. Hey, take that, fellas! Sure, most of these fans are here to cheer on the five boy wonders of 'N Sync—but they're just as psyched to see her strut her stuff onstage (after all, she is the No. 1 teen girl sensation in the country). And now that the 'N Sync tour is drawing to a close, she'll soon be making the rounds on her own. From the look and sound of things, the fans are ready.

But Brit didn't always have this enthusiastic reception. The first time she stepped onstage just a few months before, no one knew who she was. "I was really nervous," she recalled. She kept thinking of the time she went to a Backstreet Boys concert at New York City's Madison Square Garden, and the girls in the audience had practically drowned out the opening act with chants of "We want Backstreet!"

"I was worried that people wouldn't like me and that I'd forget something," she told *The Calgary Sun*. "I was really stressed, but I just got onstage and did the best I could and it turned out really well. And the more I did it, the easier it became."

The first week of the tour, she told the *San Francisco Chronicle*, was crazed. "They completely crammed my schedule and I wasn't used to the bus and everything," she admitted. She was also a little homesick—but that wore off quickly. "Once I got into it, I didn't want to go home!" she said. "I'm always on the phone with my mom and my best friends, and I get to go home every six weeks or so. When I went home for Christmas, after a week, I was like, 'I'm so bored.' "

Brit was enjoying every minute of crisscrossing the country—and learning so much. "It's been an incredible, intense time," she told *Billboard*. "It hasn't been always easy for me opening for the guys. There are all these screaming girls in the audience who came to see them. But ultimately, I win them over." And win them over she does—in only seconds. With her first "Oh, baby, baby," the crowd in Baton Rouge goes wild. "She's even more amazing in person!" exclaims one Thibodeaux, Louisiana, tenth grader. "I know her whole CD by heart."

So does everyone else, judging by the sing-along on each of the four numbers she performs. At the end of the set, she and her two dancers, Jerry and T.J., take their bows and make way for the boys. 'N Sync high-five her—she did a great job and they're proud of their gal pal.

But not every performance goes this flawlessly. Britney has had a few bloops and blunders along the tour. "Once someone threw a cupcake onstage—it was one of the girls in B*Witched's birthdays," she revealed in an online chat. While Brit was dancing, she stepped on it and slipped. T.J. had to pick her up and sweep the mess off the stage so they could continue. But Britney more than anyone knows the show must go on. "You pick yourself up, you dust yourself off," she joked when fans asked how she was feeling after the spill.

Then there are those overzealous 'N Sync fans. "Oh, my God," she told

MTV Radio Network. "The things they do! There are girls in the audience lifting up their shirts while the guys are onstage. I'm backstage dying. It's sooo bizarre!" Some have even threatened her to keep away from the 'N Sync guys. "I hear a lot of things," she told the *Kansas City Star*, "like 'Stay away from my man!' It's just a jealousy thing."

With all the extracurricular activities that come with being a successful performer—appearances, autograph sessions, interviews, the works—the few minutes before each show are just about the only time Brit and the boys have to bond. Occasionally, there's time for a meal together, but as J.C. recently explained, touring is serious business. "It's not as if we're in each other's faces all the time just playing around. We all have work to do."

"We're close—you can't be on tour night and day and not be close," Justin has said of the band's relationship with Brit. But as for all the rumors that he and she are an item? "Sorry to disappoint," he tells San Francisco reporters.

Brit chimes in, "We're friends because we worked together on the *Mickey Mouse Club* and now we're out on tour with 'N Sync—and that's as far as it goes!" Although—and she won't deny it—Justin gave her her first kiss way back when they were 'Teers together. "We were young. He was really sweet and it was fun," she has said—usually while blushing.

The Boys' Basics

Who They Are

Justin Randall Timberlake, born
    January 31, 1981, from Memphis,
    Tennessee

Chris, aka Christopher Alan
    Kirkpatrick, born October 17, 1971,
    from Pittsburgh, Pennsylvania

Joey, aka Joseph Anthony Fatone Jr.,
    born January 29, 1976, from
    Brooklyn, New York

Lance, aka James Lance Bass,
    born May 4, 1979, from Laurel,
    Mississippi

J.C., aka Joshua Scott Chasez,
    born August 8, 1976, from
    Washington, D.C.

Name Game

'N Sync comes from the last letter of
each of the guys' names (Lance's nick-
name is Lancesten—hence the N).

How It All Began

J.C. and Justin met on *MMC* in Orlando. Following the show's cancellation, the two headed for Nashville, where they shared a vocal coach while working on solo projects. They returned to Orlando (hey, if it was good enough for the Backstreet Boys), where they teamed up with Chris and Joey and began working on an act of a cappella harmonies and slick dance moves. When Lance joined up, everything came together.

Movin' On Up

They released their debut album exclusively in Europe and headed overseas to take Germany and the Netherlands by storm. Returning home in the spring of 1998, they were ready to conquer the United States Thanks to a Disney Channel special, major play on MTV, and two hit singles ("I Want You Back" and "Tearin' Up My Heart"), their album went platinum. The guys opened for

Janet Jackson before hitting the road solo and releasing a Christmas album in 1998.

What Brit Has to Say About Them

"They are all so sweet—and I've learned a lot from them. J.C. and Justin and I have known each other for like forever."

The Offical Site

www.nsync.com

Unofficial Fan Sites Worth Checking Out

www.geocities.com/SunsetStrip/
   Stadium/4721/
www.geocities.com/SunsetStrip/
   Balcony/8546
www.geocities.com/
   SunsetStrip/Frontrow/3530
www.casenet.com/people/
   nsync.htm

'N Sync Penpals
www.nsyncworld.com/
  pen/pen.html

Books to Browse
'N Sync: Tearin' Up the Charts by Matt
  Netter (Archway, 1998)
'N Sync: The Official Book by 'N Sync,
  K. M. Squires (Bantam Books, 1998)

Write to Them At
'N Sync Fan Club
P.O. Box 5248
Bellingham, WA 98227

All About B*Witched

Who They Are

Edele Lynch, Keavy Lynch, Sinead O'Carroll, Lindsay Armaou—four multitalented girls from Dublin

Claim to Fame

Their singles "C'est la Vie" and "Rollercoaster" are climbing the international charts. They've toured with 'N Sync, Boyzone, and 911. Their album, _B*witched_, hit the States in March 1999.

How They Happened

In the early eighties, twin sisters Edele and Keavy discovered a mutual love of music (it ran in their blood: Granddaddy played the fiddle) and decided to form a band. Sinead wandered into the Dublin garage where Keavy was working as a part-time mechanic, and the pair hit it off. Lindsay, who played both piano and guitar, met up with Keavy at a kick–boxing class. Presto! B*Witched was ready to cast their spell.

Sibling Rivalry
The twins' brother Shane is a member of Boyzone.

The Write Stuff
Camped out in Sinead's Dublin flat for months, they penned songs and sang into a tape recorder.

Their Groove
Part soul, part hip–hop, part traditional Irish folk. Acording to Keavy, "It's a style that's entirely our own." Critics call it pop meets *Riverdance*.

Their Style
Neon (hair, shirts, sneakers, etc.); denim (shirts, vests, jackets, capris, etc.). Fun–loving, flirty, and free . . . with a lovely Irish lilt, of course.

What Brit Has to Say About Them

"They're a lot of fun on tour and they've got a great sound."

Big Break

In concert spring 1999, on the Disney Channel

The Group's Motto

"A dream can become reality if you work for it."—Lindsay

Official Website

www.b–witched.com

Unofficial Fan Sites Worth Checking Out

www.iol.ie/~kasst/
   b–witched/index.html
www.geocities.com/Broadway/
   Stage/2226/
www.geocities.com/SunsetStrip/
   Balcony/8672/index.html

Write to Them At
B*Witched
c/o Trinity Street
3 Alveston Place
Leamington Spa
Dublin, Ireland
CV32 4BR
or e-mail them at
b–witched@b–witched.com

Hit Me One More Time . . .

To find out if 'N Sync, B*Witched, or Britney are coming to a concert arena near you, check out www.tourdates.com.

Chapter 9

❀A Diva Debuts❀

Welcome to the MTV generation, where being a talented singer isn't enough to make it in the music business. You've got to be able to translate your sound to the small screen in a showstopping production number. What do video viewers want? In general, something they can watch over and over again and never tire of ('cause chances are MTV will be running it every hour!). Something eye-catching, electrifying, even provocative. How important is a video? Let's put it this way: Without MTV, there might not have been a Madonna.

Once Britney's album was wrapped

and the single was being readied for release, it was time to make a video. The label wasn't worried one bit: Not only did Brit look great, but she had extensive acting experience. If anyone could sell it on screen, she could, and as any industry insider will tell you, a music video—no matter how many talented people are involved in its production—is only as good as the performer.

Jive hired Nigel Dick, who shot the Backstreet Boys' "As Long as You Love Me," and Britney flew to L.A. to film at Venice High School. The halls and gym looked a little familiar. That's because *Grease*, starring John Travolta and Olivia Newton-John, was shot there more than twenty years ago. Dick was enthusiastic. As far as he was concerned, Britney's ". . . Baby One More Time," would be fun, and have life, color, energy . . . and a little bit of sex.

The treatment (aka plot) was simple yet sizzling: Brit would play a kid in class, impatiently waiting for the bell to ring. The second it does, she bolts down the halls, strutting her stuff with her classmates and singing about an ex. The action moves outside, and Brit's school uniform is replaced by Spice Girl–like sweats and a hot pink crop top. She croons in the backseat of a car; does back flips beneath the palm trees; eyes a hunk in the bleachers; leads a *West Side Story*–like chorus line through the gymnasium. A teacher stares wide-eyed at the youth cutting loose before succumbing to the rhythm as well. As the bell rings again, the gang races back to class, where Brit is still daydreaming of breaking free . . . and the boy that got away.

Britney and the New York dancers had two weeks at home to rehearse before the cameras started rolling, but the L.A. group had to learn the moves in only two days. Following her, they gyrated, shimmied, even slid across the floor. It took a total of three days to film, and Dick insisted it be done in pieces, rather than as one continuous story from start to finish. This way, he reasoned, each scene would seem fresh and alive. He was right, and when it was all edited, the video flowed seamlessly. The week it debuted on MTV, it was one of the Top 5 requested videos. Brit was a hit!

Not everyone, however, was convinced the video was appropriate. Some critics questioned if the star wasn't too sexy for young, impressionable viewers. In the video, Brit wears a short skirt, thigh-high stockings, and a white shirt tied to bare her belly. "She has a wholesome image, but the image on the video is far from innocent," says Danya Harpster of *The Times-Picayune*, who interviewed Britney in January 1999. "It's very seductive, a completely different message than what her CD cover—and Britney herself in interviews—projects."

"It would be different if I was walking around naked," Brit defended herself during an AOL chat. "But where I'm from, I don't think anything if someone has a sports bra on and is dancing. It's just fun. It's not like I'm trying to be too sexy. Anyone who knows me will tell you, that's just not my style."

No negative word, however, could stop Britney's single from burning up the charts. By the time her album hit stores in mid-January, fans were dying to hear what else the red-hot singer had to offer. If there had been any doubt that she was more than a one-hit wonder, the reviews now confirmed what Jive had known all along: Britney's debut album, critics agreed almost unanimously, was sophisticated, soulful . . . and not just kid stuff.

<u>*What the Reviews Have to Say*</u>

"Spears's voice is perky and pleasant and her delivery capable. She's a seasoned show–biz pro, so it's no surprise that every catch in her throat, ever quasi–soul riff is expertly hewn."
    —Joan Anderman, *The Boston Globe*

"Spears' approach certainly has struck a chord. Her initial single shot up the charts on impact in December, whetting fans' appetites so much that her album debuted at No. 1."
    —Jim Farber, *New York Daily News*

"An energetically wholesome, aggressively marketed 17–year–old from small–town Louisiana, Spears epitomizes the modern idol aesthetic ... entertaining, accessible and slickly packaged."
    —J. D. Considine, *The Baltimore Sun*

"She is an excellent dancer in a Paula Abdul kind of way, and projects an innocent allure, albeit ... one closer to Lolita than Disney."
—David E. Thigpen, *Time*

"Spears, a mix of Debbie Gibson's wholesomeness and Alanis Morissette's grit, has unseated boy bands 'N Sync and Backstreet Boys as the hottest act in the exploding teen music market."
—*People*

"A step up from those Spicey babes, she's a stronger singer than Sporty, Scary, etc. And ... *Baby One More Time* is a more consistent album than either of the projects those Spicemeisters have given us so far."
—Tom Roland, *The Tennessean*

"The 17-year-old sings about the usual—boys, love, breakups—but you'll be too busy dancing to upbeat tunes to ponder her lyrics. If pop is your thing, Britney Spears will get you going."

—*Seventeen*

"You knew it was coming: the sassy girl backlash to that whole 'N Sync/Backstreet Boys testosterone-lite thing. Hanging ten on the sugary wave is 17-year-old ex-Disney princess Britney Spears, who sounds so soulful and Whitney-assured, it's downright scary."

—Tom Lanham, *Entertainment Weekly*

"She brings a fresh-faced girl-next-door appeal. The spunky puppy-love title track already bubbled up to the Top 5, and there's plenty more fizz where that came from."

—*USA Today*

The Perks of Being a Pop Star

With diva status comes privilege.
Britney:

- rides around in limos and lives in a
  Jive corporate apartment in NYC.
- carries a cell phone for keeping in
  touch with Mom and best buds
  any time of day.
- gets to be primped and pampered
  by star stylists for a *Teen People* shoot
  (they gave her a head–to–toe make-
  over, complete with hair extensions
  and glam makeup).
- models gorgeous designer clothes
  from Vivienne Tam, BCBG, and
  Todd Oldham.
- shops in super–trendy New York
  City's SoHo, while salespeople wait
  on her every whim (at Scoop, one
  salesgirl held armfuls of outfits
  while Brit scoped out the racks).
- sat next to Whitney Houston (her
  idol), rubbed elbows with Julia
  Roberts and Prince, and introduced

the Goo–Goo Dolls at the American Music Awards.

- was fawned over (and offered a Ring Ding) by Rosie O'Donnell on her talk show.
- hung with *90210*'s Vincent Young ("I nearly died!"), *Felicity*'s Keri Russell, Lil' Kim, and the casts of *Buffy*, *Sabrina*, and *Boy Meets World* at an anniversary bash for *Teen People*.
- travels first–class around the world to promote her album. So far, L.A. and Singapore have been her favorite spots.

Brit Brain Buster 3: Her Video

1. Who is the video's producer?
   a. Babyface
   b. Britney Spears
   c. Dawson Leery
   d. Nina D'luhy

2. Approximately how many minutes does the video run?
   a. 3:55
   b. 2:00
   c. 7:04
   d. 5:05

3. What is the first image you see of
   Britney?
   a. doing a back flip
   b. dancing by the lockers
   c. tapping her loafer
   d. drumming her pen on the
      desk

4. Which of the following outfits
   does Britney *not* wear?
   a. a school uniform

    b. pink crop top
    c. gray ribbed cardigan
    d. yellow hooded sweatshirt

5. The color of the convertible she croons in is:
    a. bubble gum pink
    b. electric blue
    c. red–hot red
    d. jet black

6. The name of the high school team printed on the gym wall is:
    a. Kentwood High Vultures
    b. Rydell High Ravens
    c. Venice High Gondoliers
    d. Spears Central Sparrows

7. The letter written on the gym floor is:
    a. B
    b. S
    c. Z
    d. V

8. The boy in the bleachers checking Brit out is:
   a. her cousin
   b. her big brother
   c. her ex–boyfriend
   d. Justin Timberlake

9. Who is the teacher jammin' in the gym?
   a. Britney's mom
   b. Britney's kindergarten teacher
   c. a friend of the family from Kentwood
   d. Hillary Clinton

10. Who edited the video?
    a. Britney
    b. Justin and J.C.
    c. Susan Agostinelli
    d. Declan Whitebloom

Answers:

1. d; 2. a; 3. c; 4. d; 5. b; 6. c; 7. d; 8. a; 9. c; 10. d

<u>*Translation, Please?*</u>

Sorry, there are no Cliffs Notes (yet!) to Britney's poignant lyrics. So in case you're too busy grooving to try to comprehend the message behind the music, read on:

"... Baby One More Time"

Synopsis: Girlfriend was clueless about how much she loved her man ... until he was out that door. Now she's moaning and wishing they could rekindle the flames.

The dilemma: What's a girl to do when he's history? Seems the protagonist has been spending all her nights alone, trying to figure out how she blew it. She's got it bad, even claiming he's the reason for her being. All he has to do is say the word and she'll be back.

Conclusion: The sad, sad truth? You don't know what you got till it's gone.

"Sometimes"

Synopsis: Another relationship gone awry. Again, the miss in the music seems to have done the wrong thing. She's got some serious intimacy issues—the minute he gets close, she pulls away. But she's not willing to kiss it goodbye just yet and tries to explain how she feels about falling head over heels.

The dilemma: Romeo wants to rush things, but this heroine likes things at her own speed.

Conclusion: Anything good is worth waiting for.

"Born to Make You Happy"

Synopsis: Regrets are all this chick has left of her failed romance. She mopes in her room, crying over his picture, before resolving to go on with her life. In her heart, she believes they're meant to be together, soul mates destined to reunite if only they could meet once more and talk over their differences.

Dilemma: Should you get thee to a nunnery or rejoin the human race?

Conclusion: Past is just that—past. You can't spend your life living a dream.

"From the Bottom of My Broken Heart"

Synopsis: They've called it quits, and it wasn't a pretty scene. She begged; he bailed. So now she's moving on and he's with someone new. Will she get over it? Not completely. He'll always hold a special place in her heart. True love does that to you.

The dilemma: How do you deal when your guy is way over you and you're still hooked on him?

Conclusion: Time to close the ex–files. Bygones.

Hit Me One More Time . . .

For a behind-the-scenes look at how videos are put together, check out *You Stand There: Making Music Video* by David Kleiler and Robert Moses (Three Rivers Press, 1997).

Chapter 10

✤She's Got
the Look✤

Those lips ... those eyes ... those killer clothes. Don't hate her because she's beautiful. The brains behind Brit's sizzling style say *anyone* can copy her look—with a little inside information, of course.

"Britney's still a kid, so her look is still evolving," says Rudy Sotomayor, who did her makeup for *Teen People* and several of the shots on her CD. "She's willing to try new things, and she loves to look grown-up, sophisticated, and sexy." Brit liked his handiwork so much, Sotomayor has become her steady makeup artist for New York City appearances. "She calls me a lot—I've done her for MTV as well as

115

Rosie O'Donnell—and we've become friends. I just adore her," he says. "Some stars come with an attitude—they think they know it all. But Brit puts her face in your hands."

Rudy Reveals: Brit's Baby Doll Look

Just like the one you see on her album cover—soft, sheer, sweet, and oh so au naturel. "This look is perfect for school days and casual weekends," Sotomayor says. "It's so light and clean, it looks like you're wearing no makeup at all. All you see is a healthy glow."

Foundation: Apply a sheer, light moisturizing base to the face, blending with a sponge. Don't forget to extend the color down the neck to create a seamless look.

Brows: Using powder (eyebrow or eye shadow color is fine) and a stiff, angled brush, fill in brows with a color one shade lighter than your own. "Don't go too dark or it will look too severe," Sotomayor advises. He actually lightened Brit's brows for *Teen People*, using Jolene bleach (to match her honey-colored hair). "It opened up her whole face and gave her a much softer, more flattering look."

Eyes: Cover the entire eyelid with a soft beige shadow, blending well with a soft brush or sponge applicator. For more sparkle, you can choose a frostier shade, but keep it light and sheer. Apply one coat of mascara.

Cheeks: A coral blush applied just to the apple of the cheeks makes Brit look rosy but real. "Choose a neutral shade, like tawny—nothing too pink, nothing too orange, but somewhere in between," Sotomayor advises. "People won't be able to tell if you're wearing makeup or just blushing naturally."

Lips: Kiss flat matte shades goodbye. Opt instead for tinted glosses that give you a wet, sexy look. "Light pinks, peaches, and nudes with lots of shine are what I use on Britney," he says. "The color is very feminine and delicate, but the dewiness is seductive."

Brands he used on Brit: Benefit, Tony & Tina (available at Urban Outfitters and other stores), MAC (foundation), Estée Lauder (blush).

Rudy Reveals: Brit's Bad Girl Look

"Sizzle and sex appeal—that's what this face is all about," says Sotomayor. You know the steamy styles he means: smoky eyes, pouty lips, shimmering cheeks. "She likes this look for concerts and for talk shows, and she chose it for the cover of her CD in Europe and Japan. There's nothing teenybopper about it." Though it's way too dramatic for daytime, you can choose this palette for evenings out or even prom night, "any occasion where you need to stop traffic."

Foundation: Again, go with a sheer moisturizing base all over. Says Sotomayor, "Applying foundation is like preparing a clean canvas for a painting. It makes your skin look flawless."

Brows: Work with a shade that matches the color of your brows and emphasize the arch—it helps shape your whole face. Apply powder with a stiff, angled brush.

Eyes: Choose charcoal shadows or smoky browns and apply only to the bottom part of the lid, smudging softly. Then apply a white or peach highlight to the brow bone and blend the two shades. Add mascara and a touch of the dark shadow beneath the lower lashes for more drama.

Cheeks: Apply a blush that has a shimmering frost or sparkle to the cheekbones. "Brit is a girl who goes for glitter," he says.

Lips: When the emphasis is on your eyes, you want to downplay your mouth. Sotomayor uses a matte nude shade on Britney's lips. "That way you are just drawn to her sexy gaze—and nothing stands in the way."

Brand he used on Brit: Vincent Longo (baby love collection for eyes and cheeks; lipstick).

Hair flair: On the *Teen People* shoot, hairstylist Matthew Williams took Brit to new lengths with hair extensions. "She looked so sophisticated," Sotomayor recalls. "And she loved it so much, she's been keeping it up. She wears it straight most of the time; crimped for special occasions like award shows. And the color is softer and more ethereal as well: chunky blond highlights mixed with her own caramel color."

Dressed to Impress:
Brit's Wicked Wardrobe

"She's got it and she likes to flaunt it," says Danny Flynn, the Cloutier stylist who clothed Britney for her spring 1999 *Entertainment Weekly* cover with 'N Sync. "It was one of her first big magazine layouts, and she wanted to look amazing."

Not too tough a task: The girl has abs of steel and a figure that would make Demi Moore green with envy. "She's busty," Flynn says. "But she's also petite and about a size six. That combination really works wonders for a wardrobe."

Pink was the color of choice—not just because it's the hot shade this season, but because it's youthful and fun, and complements Brit's peaches-and-cream complexion. "It's very bubble gum, which is teen pop's image," Flynn says. On the *EW* cover, she wears a flirty pink floral skirt (baring her belly button, of course!) and a stretchy tube top in tomato red. Inside, she's white hot in capris and a big button-down shirt (with a black bra peeking out from underneath), with pink stiletto sandals.

"In her final shot, I had her in a pink tank that said 'Cherry Bomb' on it, pink capris, and silver sequin heels. She looked young, but I don't know about innocent!"

Brit was open to trying new colors, fabrics, and designers, Flynn says. "I think she got inspired to go out and buy some of them herself. She confided in me that she's a total shopaholic—her closets at home are overflowing." Like most teens, Brit tends to go for the trends. "But as she matures, she's becoming more secure in her own tastes and trusting her instincts."

When *Rolling Stone* put her in a revealing satin Wonderbra and Frederick's of Hollywood hot pants for its April 15, 1999 cover, she didn't even bat an eyelash.

"She has great confidence about her body, which is a rarity among teenage girls," says Flynn. "And the golden rule of style is this: if you think you look great, so will the rest of the world."

What Danny had her don: a good push-up bra (cleavage counts!), cute cutoff or tube tops, athletic warm-up pants or capris, killer heels.

Labels he liked (and so did Brit): Urban Outfitters, NYSE, Curve, Jill Stewart, Smashing Grandpa, Tommy Hilfiger.

Other designer duds you'll spot her in: Vivienne Tam, BCBG Max Azria, Miu Miu, So Hip It Hurts, Diesel, Donna Karan, Calvin Klein.

What? No Prom Date?

With her sexy new style, the boys are certainly beating down her door (some have shown up at concerts with signs that read "Marry me, Britney!") but fellas, did someone forget to invite Brit to the prom this year?

"No one has asked me," she recently

told *Teen Celebrity Style*. "I guess everyone knows that I'm a little busy." Even with her hectic schedule, she'd never turn down an invitation from Brad Pitt or Ben Affleck. "Oh my god," she gushed on *Access Hollywood*. "I know Brad has Jennifer Aniston, but I'm here if he wants to call me!"

Should Brad be unable to oblige, what exactly is her ideal prom pick? "Hard-to-get kind of guys—the ones who play it cool and you don't know what they're thinking," she told WEOW radio in Key West, Florida. "Hey, no wonder no one asked me out!"

Are You a Bit Brit? A Style Quiz

1. Your idea of a comfy weekend outfit is:
   a. a tiny tank from A/X and faded jeans
   b. a frilly floral sundress and strappy sandals
   c. khakis and a sweater

2. The new 'do you'll likely sport this season is:
   a. a short spiky crop
   b. pigtails with funky feathered holders
   c. an elegant French braid

3. Your toes are always tapping in:
   a. neon high tops
   b. chunky loafers
   c. Birkenstocks

4. Your favorite jewelry is:
   a. an armful of thin bangle bracelets

b. a string of pearls
c. a bold gold brooch

5. Your favorite designers are:
   a. Dior, Prada, and Hermès
   b. your own home-sewn fashions
   c. Tommy Hilfiger, bebe, and
      Betsey Johnson

Answers:
1. a; 2. b; 3. b; 4. a; 5. c.

How You Scored

All 5: You and Brit should hit the malls together. You two couldn't be more style simpatico.

3–4: There's definitely a bit of Brit in you. You love her flirtatious, funky look, but mix it with your own tastes as well.

1–2: It's doubtful you'd ever win a Britney Spears look-alike contest. You love her music, but her ensembles aren't exactly your cup of tea.

O: You and Brit would never see eye to eye on fashion. But hey, give her style a chance to grow on you. Watch her video a dozen more times for some inspiration.

Hit Me One More Time . . .

- To contact Britney, write the Britney Fan Club, P.O. Box 7022, Red Bank, NJ 07701–7022 or e-mail her at Britney@peeps.com.
- Her official website is www.peeps.com/britney.
- To follow Brit's progress on the charts (can double platinum be far away?), check out Billboard On-line at www.billboard.com. You can view the Top 100 positions as well as all the latest music news.

Chapter 11

✸Future Perfect✸

"It's nice to know,
after all this hard work,
people really appreciate it.
It's a really good feeling."
—BRITNEY TO BILLBOARD, OCTOBER 1998

In the several months since Britney burst onto the pop scene, her phone has been ringing off the hook with offers. Everyone from clothing designers to fast-food restaurants wants a piece of her. Why? Because she's America's new teen sweetheart, and anything she touches turns to solid gold (better make that platinum!).

She's said yes to many things—covers

of magazines, talk shows including *Donny & Marie* and *Live! With Regis & Kathie Lee*, and a $5 million ad campaign for Tommy Hilfiger jeans. The clothing company firmly believes its audience is the same one that watches MTV—so you know they'd love to see Britney wearing their red, white, and blue logo on a billboard.

"His clothes are really simple but funky," Britney has said of Hilfiger's line. In fact, at a New York City photo shoot for the ad, she was psyched to wear some of the outfits off-camera. "I can't wait to go to the Hilfiger office," she told *People.* "I am totally getting so many clothes!"

Along with Brit, Tommy ads will reportedly feature R&B artist Mya, thirteen-year-old Puff Daddy protégé Jerome Childers, Rapper Q-Tip, and DJ Mark Ronson. And the designer label may sponsor some upcoming concert tours as well—maybe even Britney's. Fans got a glimpse of the first shots—Brit singing in a studio—in an ad spread in *Teen People,*

YM magazine, and other publications in spring 1999. In the three photos, she's wearing a cute white tank and dark blue jeans and singing into a microphone during a session. A stars-and-stripes electric guitar with a Tommy Hilfiger logo rests against a piano in the corner.

According to the *New York Post*, this may be only the first of a long line of commercial deals for Britney. She signed on as the newest face of the Company modeling agency, where boss Michael Flutie will have her doing "special endorsements."

There has also been a great deal of talk about Brit getting back into acting. She told several interviewers she had been to lunch with the producer of WB's *Dawson's Creek* and would be shooting three episodes of the series. One of the show's stars, Josh Jackson, who plays Pacey, squashed those rumors on a recent MTV *Total Request Live*. When host Carson Daly asked Josh about Britney, he said he knew nothing about it. And at that time, there were only two episodes left to be filmed for the season, and Britney was not slated to be in them. The show's publicity office confirms that *Dawson's Creek*'s creative team did indeed meet Brit and was bowled over by her. There are tentative plans for her to be on next season, but that won't begin filming until late summer 1999. "I won't play somebody mean, and I won't play myself," she told *Entertainment Weekly* in March.

EW also recently reported Brit's actually cut a development deal with Columbia TriStar Television—the production company behind *Dawson's Creek* and *Party of Five*—to star in her own series. Brit's looking to land a drama, not a sitcom, and Columbia has eighteen months to pitch her a show to her liking. Even if she does flip for one script, cameras won't roll till after she releases her next album—and that's not happening till spring 2000.

Britney's future will certainly depend on the choices she makes—the people she chooses to work with, the songs she records, and the way she lets herself be marketed. Everyone is confident she has a good head on her shoulders and will think things through carefully.

"If she wants to stay on top, she needs to keep challenging herself as an artist and challenging what people think and know about her," says *Billboard*'s Chuck Taylor. "She can be wholesome, she can be sexy. She's tremendously versatile, and that's where staying power comes from."

Britney, he adds, has also not let the attention go to her head. "She's not the artist on high," Taylor says. "She goes out into the small towns and signs autographs, she sings in the malls. She's accessible, just one of the girls—and that's smart marketing."

"It's all up to her," insists *The Times-Picayune*'s Danya Harpster. "She seems to have a very realistic view of it all—she's not going to get caught up in believing all her hype. And she's a normal kid from a good family, and that's the best foundation any artist starting out can have."

Britney is also no fool when it comes to

understanding the fickle CD-buying public. "I want to go to college one day so I have a backup," she announced on America Online. "Right now I want to focus on my music, but I know this business is crazy. I definitely want something to fall back on."

And it's that same crazy music business which prevents her from dating anytime soon (she is, after all, a red-blooded American teenager!). While the idea of romance is appealing, a guy would have to be very understanding of Britney's demanding professional life. "With me on the road, there has to be a major amount of trust," she told *People*. Besides, she confided, until she meets the man of her dreams (and she's open for offers from anyone fitting the description of Prince Charming), she's head over heels in love with . . . her job.

This summer, she'll be traveling overseas to the UK, Germany, Holland, France, and Scandinavia, promoting her album on foreign TV. In the States, she'll be formulating her own tour (perhaps as early as a summer 1999 start-up) and making the talk-show rounds, including *The Tonight Show* with Jay Leno. All of these activities had to be postponed for over a month when she twisted her knee on February 11, 1999, during dance rehearsals for her second video, "Sometimes," in Malibu. The injury was initially thought to be minor, but when it swelled so much on a photo shoot later that week (the leg of her pants would barely fit), doctors decided that she had to undergo arthroscopic surgery. Dr. Tim Finney, the chief doctor for the New Orleans Saints, removed a small piece of loose cartilage through three minor incisions. Brit recuperated at Doctors' Hospital in New Orleans for a few days and was ordered to rest up—and lay off the dancing or even walking—for five weeks at home in Kentwood. "I'm itchy to get back to work and I wish it was healing quicker," she told *Access Hollywood*. "But the fans have been so great in supporting me and sending me get-well cards—that's helped my spirits a lot."

Brit was brokenhearted over the delay, but vowed she'll make up for it. "I've been working nonstop touring since September," she said in a released statement from her record company. "I'm really sad to be missing all these great television shows and the opportunity to see how everyone will react to my performance, but I guess this is just my body's way of telling me I need a break."

By April, she was back on track with Nigel Dick, working on the "Sometimes" video, timed to the release of her second single. "(You Drive Me) Crazy" is slated to be her third single, in stores this summer.

"I've been working toward this moment for a long time," she told MTV. "I just want to keep on building and building, doing more and more."

And the world can't wait to see what more is in store for Britney Spears.

Did You Catch Her . . .

- modeling prom dresses in the March 1999 issue of *Teen?*
- on the cover of *Smile* magazine?
- on the cover of *Rolling Stone* hugging a Teletubbie?
- as a presenter on the American Music Awards and in the audience at the Grammy Awards?
- singing her heart out on *Donny & Marie, The Howie Mandel Show, The Ricki Lake Show,* Fox Family Network's *The Countdown Show,* Nickelodeon's *All That, The Rosie O'Donnell Show,* and *Live! With Regis & Kathie Lee?*
- at her happy Louisiana homecoming on MTV News's *1515?*
- on Electric Circus (MuchMusic) in Toronto, Ontario?
- on *E! News Weekend* (they showed a clip of her on *Star Search*)?
- on *Motown Live?*
- as spokesperson for the Just Nikki catalog?

- doing a milk ad (white mustache and all)?
- performing Grad Night at Walt Disney World?
- in articles/photos in *Vogue*, *People*, *Teen People*, *Teen Celebrity Style*, *Girl's Life*, *Teen*, *Jump*, and *Seventeen*?
- being reviewed in *SPIN*, *Rolling Stone*, *Entertainment Weekly*, *Time*, *Interview*, *USA Today*, *New York Post*, and *Billboard*?
- chatting up a storm with fans on America Online's Entertainment Asylum? (If you missed it, check out the transcripts: Keyword BRITNEY.)
- cohosting YTV's *Hit List* in Canada?
- at Benetton and Calvin Klein in New York City, the Oxford Valley Mall in Langhorn, Pennsylvania, and the Mall of America in Bloomington, Minnesota?
- at Q102's Jingle Ball in Philadelphia with Taylor Dayne, LFO, All Saints, Divine, and Le Click?

Her Resolutions for the Future

To quit worrying: "I lie in bed at night and I'll just think of the stupidest things," she told MTV Online. "I'm so paranoid."

To break bad habits: "I'll stop biting my nails," she added. "It's so ugly!"

To get creative: "I want to write some music and experiment with new sounds, things I've never tried before," she told the _Minneapolis Star and Tribune._ "That's how you grow."

To become a screen (or scream) queen: "I'll always have music in my life," she told _The Times-Picayune_, "but I would like to get into some films if I could ... stuff the teenagers can relate to. Like Jennifer Love Hewitt or Neve Campbell movies."

To stay her sweet self: "I don't think fame will change me," she told the _San_

Beth Peters

Francisco Chronicle. "I'm no different than I was when I started out in this business. I'm still Britney Spears from Kentwood, Louisiana."

To encourage kids: "I think the reason I am where I am is because I had people who believed in me," she said in a recent online chat. "It would be nice if I could inspire some young kids to sing, dance, act, too."

140

What's in Her Stars?

Her sign: Born December 2, Brit is a Sagittarius (November 22–December 21).

Celebs who share her birthday: Opera diva Maria Callas, French impressionist painter Georges Seurat, tennis champ Monica Seles, actress Julie Harris.

What her sign says about her: Those born under Sag tend to be wanderers and truth-seekers who enjoy hitting the road and looking for the meaning of life. The symbol for this sign is the centaur (half man, half beast) pulling a bow and arrow. Centaurs were the intellectuals of ancient mythology, and Sagittarians are likely to be clear thinkers as well. Being skilled archers, they tend to get straight to the point in any conversation. Sags never mince words.

Sag strengths: Curious, dynamic, exploring, generous, bold, bright.

Sag weaknesses: Temperamental, aggressive, judgmental, outspoken.

Personality traits: Sagittarians have tremendous spirit and drive and an insatiable thirst for knowledge. They are gifted at evaluating situations and viewing the big picture. But on the negative side, they can be blunt and argumentative when people disagree with their very strong opinions.

Planetary rules: Sagittarius is ruled by the planet Jupiter. In ancient Roman times, Jupiter was the king of the gods, and Sagittarians are likely to have a regal air about them as well. Like Brit, many Sagittarian ladies love winning crowns in contests and thrive on applause and adulation.

Fired up: The element linked to Sagittarius is fire, and like a flame, Sags tend to flit from one thing to another without ever looking back. Brit is also likely a fast talker, naturally athletic, and fiery tempered.

Lucky lady: Like a typical Sag, Brit may be quick to take a gamble on things, feeling both lucky and smart. Things come so easily to those born under this sign, thanks to their charming nature and talent.

Career obstacles: The next year brings new beginnings and unexpected oppositions. This is clearly Britney's time to shine, with phenomenal success (yes, even more!) looming on the horizon. The only hitch? She may find her advisers disagreeing with her when it comes to the direction she wants to take. She'll have to speak her mind and stand her ground to convince them she's right (even if she's only seventeen, she's wise beyond her years). If she follows her keen intuition, her star will continue to blaze.

Wherefore art thou, Romeo? Just as she says, this career-minded girl will put romance on the back burner for a while. Sure, she'll meet lots of cute and eligible guys at social functions (sparking endless tabloid rumors, no doubt), but none of them will hold her interest for very long. Brit will likely just flirt, then flee.

Give me a break: A vacation is likely this year, perhaps to an exotic locale. Brit will need time off after touring and promoting to rejuvenate body and soul.

Hit Me One More Time . . .

- To find stores that sell Brit's hot Hilfiger outfit, you can contact Tommy Hilfiger U.S.A., Inc., 25 West 39th Street, New York, NY 10018.
- Watch for word of a Brit guest–starring role at the official *Dawson's Creek* website, www.dawsonscreek.com

*Please read on
for a sneak peek at*

The Heat Is On
98°

by Leah and Elina Furman

Published by Ballantine Books
Available in August 1999

Setting the
World on Fire!

From Manila to Canada, from the Philippines to the United Kingdom, 98 Degrees has been blazing a fiery trail of R & B madness, bringing their soulful harmonies to an army of loyal fans prepared to lay down their lives for any one of the attractive young crooners. At every stop of their grueling touring schedule, they are met by throngs of screeching admirers, straining their necks for a mere glimpse of the famed Ohio quartet. And who could blame them? After only a month in stores, their second album, *98 Degrees and Rising*, went gold in the United States, Asia, and Canada. And the album's unforgettable second single, "Because of You," has skyrocketed into the platinum stratosphere.

But before the platinum and gold singles . . . before the fan frenzy . . . before the worldwide touring and round-the-clock photo shoots, before the numerous television and radio show appearances, 98 Degrees was just a figment of one young man's imagination. He is Jeff Timmons, founding father of 98 Degrees.

The four young members of 98 Degrees—Jeff Timmons, Justin Jeffre, Nick Lachey, and Drew Lachey—paid their dues a long time before they caught their first big break. From delivering Chinese takeout to protecting Los Angeles's velvet-rope social scene as nightclub bouncers, these boys had to bide their time, patiently waiting for the chance to show the world what they were really made of—and show us they did.

Ever since the release of their self-titled debut album in the summer of 1997, the fabulous foursome seemed destined to rise to the top of the charts. With the success of their first-ever hit single, "Invisible Man," the world waited with bated breath for an equally powerful follow-up. But, inevitably, breaking into the mainstream would take some time. Not ones to be complacent, the band members took matters into their own hands by heating up their repertoire with deeper melodies and sharper moves. Today, the young singers are living proof that perseverance, hard work, and patience really do pay off.

Worshiped for their hypnotic voices, smoldering good looks, and passionate lyrics, these guys proved themselves to be genuine artists, capable of writing soulful ballads that bridge all cultures and all ages. Unlike some bands, manufactured by powerful studio executives and managers, these boys knew each other long before becoming the phenomenon known as 98 Degrees. All hailed from Ohio, but each took a detour before making their collective climb up the charts.

While Drew was hard at work building his career as an emergency medical technician in New York, Nick and Justin were playing small gigs while attending separate colleges in Cincinnati. It would take L.A.-based Jeff's foresight and vision to finally bring all the members together. Countless rehearsals, small-venue performances, and rejections later, the boys were finally discovered by current manager Paris D'John at a Boyz II Men concert. Soon after, Motown got wind of their demo tape and instantly offered them a record contract.

As the only white group ever signed to the legendary Motown label, the band mates felt a keen obligation to succeed. Following in the footsteps of such musical greats as the Four Tops, the Temptations, and the Supremes, 98 Degrees had their work cut out for them. But the challenge only motivated them to work harder, longer, and faster.

Having traversed the globe for several months, the band was finally ready to launch its U.S. tour in the fall of 1998. Although they had enjoyed only moderate success winning over mainstream tastes before, they would have no such problems this time around.

The subjects of too many websites to count and the recipients of too many fan letters to answer personally, the band members are still trying to cope with their fans' unceasing appreciation and support. Filled with everything from sexy lingerie to handmade trinkets, their fan mail is bursting with phone numbers, glamorous photos, and desperate pleas for just one date. But as most fans have already learned, they'll need to get in line because the 98 Degrees syndrome has been spreading like wildfire and burning up hearts around the world.

Not that they aren't grateful for the adulation. Each band member has personally vowed his undying loyalty to every fan who has helped make their careers a success. To keep up their end of the bargain, the group regularly reveals juicy tidbits about their lives in such magazines as *Teen*, *Seventeen*, *Teen People*, and *YM*. Holding steady at the top of the charts with the help of a stylin' new video, and collaborating with some of the industry's biggest heavyweights—including Fugees members Wyclef Jean and Pras, and the producers of Mariah Carey, Ace of Base, and Will Smith—the band is looking forward to making even greater strides in the years to come.

Late in 1998, the quartet recorded a track with veteran musician Stevie Wonder for the soundtrack of the animated movie *Mulan*. Next, they appeared in a lineup of crowd-pleasing performances in the Macy's Thanksgiving Day parade, on *The View*, *The Howie Mandel Show*, *Loveline*, and Jay Leno's show. On top of all that, the guys were even asked to make a guest appearance on *City Guys*, an NBC comedy series. Singing, dancing, and now acting? Is there anything these guys can't do?

Whatever 98 Degrees touches seems to turn gold, and sometimes even platinum. You can be sure that their story, their dreams, and their wild journey to the top of the music industry will leave you breathless and wanting more. If you think these guys can't get any hotter, watch out, because they've only just begun to turn up the heat!

Just the Four of Us

Although every member of 98 Degrees originally hails from Ohio, it took the guys a long time to join forces and get on their way to becoming one of the hottest singing sensations to date. They may have been geographically close in their early years, but when the boys grew up, each member branched off to pursue his own personal dreams.

It may be hard to believe, but neither Jeff, Drew, Nick, nor Justin ever envisioned a successful singing career in his future. Although music had always been their first love, all of them had made other plans for their lives. Not that we could blame them. With their trusty high-school diplomas in hand, going to college to receive an education was a most level-headed option. From rescuing heart-attack victims to studying psychology, these boys set realistic goals for their future, picking stable careers that would make them a comfortable living.

As luck would have it, all of that changed very soon. Thanks to Jeff Timmons, the founding father of 98 Degrees, each guy eventually set his course for Los Angeles. And after a whole lot of trials, tribulations, and memorable moments, 98 Degrees was finally ready to hit the big time. But as success is something that rarely happens overnight, the guys still enjoy a good laugh when they think about what they went through prior to becoming famous. They all agree that their persistence and strength got them where they are today.

It took several years and many lineup changes for the boys to finally begin rehearsing, touring, and recording as a group. During that time, three members jumped ship, unwilling to make the necessary sacrifices. Of course, they're probably kicking themselves right now for bailing so early in the game. And who wouldn't? When one considers all the fame, fortune, and respect the boys of 98 Degrees have garnered, it seems that keeping the group together was well worth the tremendous effort.

Explaining the story of how Drew, Jeff, Nick, and Justin got together is much like trying to recite the course of a TV miniseries: It's a long winding tale, full of thrilling events and difficult moments. The abridged version goes as follows: Jeff formed a vocal group with three other guys . . . when two dropped out, he was left alone with Jonathan, who knew Nick from school ... Jonathan called Nick, who got on the phone and called Justin ... Nick and Justin joined ... then Jonathan dropped out ... then Nick and Justin called Nick's baby brother, Drew ... when Drew joined up, it was Jeff, Nick, Justin, and Drew ... they called themselves Just Us. Confused? Well, you should be. Because it'll take a lot more than a short description to reveal the full struggle and depth of emotion that went into the making of 98 Degrees.

The Man with the Plan

Jeff Timmons may seem like your average, run-of-the-mill heartthrob, who likes to play sports, meet girls, and hang out. But while everyone else was having fun and enjoying themselves, Jeff was hatching a plan that would forever change the course of his life.

When he first considered starting a vocal group, Jeff had no idea what he was getting into, or whether he had what it took to reach his goal. But behind every great idea stands an even greater person—exactly the kind of person Jeff was and is today. Committed to his cause, he withstood criticism, insults, and setbacks to turn his dreams into reality. Any true-blue 98 Degrees fan should know that it was Jeff Timmons who was responsible for luring his friends away from their conventional lifestyles. It was Jeff who persuaded Justin, Nick, and Drew to trade stability and financial success for a life on the fringe of the music industry. But how did he manage such a feat? Did he know something no one else did?

While studying psychology at Kent State University in Ohio was gratifying, Jeff couldn't help but feel that something was missing from his life. Since college life had its own set of perks—independence, parties, and cool classes—Jeff enjoyed campus living. No one could have suspected that he would one day leave it all behind.

With plans to become a professional football player, Jeff seemed to have it all together. "I never even dreamed about being a singer, ever," Jeff remembered. "I wanted to be a pro football player, that's what my goal was, until I decided to become a singer a few years ago."

Everything was going according to plan, when Jeff set out for a college party that would turn his life upside down. While mingling the night away, he and some friends decided to serenade a group of girls they'd had their eyes on. But while Jeff had only been hoping for a date, he got a lot more than he expected. To his utter amazement, the girls didn't laugh at him. Instead, they went wild for his singing and demanded an encore right on the spot. Basking in the glow of this attention, Jeff proceeded to belt out several ditties for his new fans' enjoyment. When the party started winding down, it was all he and his college buddies could do to escape with their shirts intact.

Feeling giddy from his success, Jeff realized he had something special. He'd always known he could sing, but this was unbelievable. He had never thought that anyone would actually beg him to belt out a tune. Unwilling to part with the warm rush of feelings that accompanied him home from the party that night, Jeff decided he would quit school and pursue his passion. To keep second thoughts at bay, he began packing his bags the very next day. He scrapped all his ideas of tackling the NFL and graduating college. Jeff had heard the call and responded by going to Los Angeles to try his luck as a performer.

With its sandy beaches, blond women, and fun nightlife, the City of Angels was the place to be. Upon his arrival in 1995, Jeff was quickly won over by the allure of Los Angeles. But before he could really enjoy what the town had to offer, Jeff was intent on bringing together his new singing group. After meeting with dozens of young men, Jeff finally found the threesome he needed to complete his ensemble. They called themselves Just Us.

During that time, Jeff did like an Angelino and took on some acting jobs just to make ends meet. One of these was a commercial for the U.S. Navy. While many struggling actors would gladly have traded places with Jeff, he wasn't about to quit chasing his dream. Convinced that with some work and dedication his vocal group would become a huge success, Jeff poured all of his creative energy into music.

Sadly, recognition wasn't in the cards. After six months of hard work with nothing to show for it, two members deserted the Just Us camp for good. "I went through all these ads and I couldn't find the right people," Jeff told *BigBopper* magazine. While most of us would have thrown in our microphones at that point, the setback only spurred Jeff on. Almost immediately, he began looking to fill the vacant slots with new members—he was that committed to making it work.

To read more about the fabulous foursome, including individual profiles, get *The Heat Is On: 98°*